The Joy of Schubert, Schumann and Mendelssohn

**A colorful, romantic repertory of their easier piano masterpieces.
Selected and arranged by Denes Agay.**

Cover design by Mike Bell Design, London

Order No. YK 21834
US International Standard Book Number: 0.8256.8102.2
UK International Standard Book Number: 0.7119.6761.X

Exclusive Distributors:
Music Sales Corporation
257 Park Avenue South, New York, NY 10010 USA
Music Sales Limited
8/9 Frith Street, London W1V 5TZ England
Music Sales Pty. Limited
120 Rothschild Street, Rosebery, Sydney, NSW 2018, Australia

Printed in the United States of America by
Vicks Lithograph and Printing Corporation

Yorktown Music Press, Inc.
New York/London/Sydney

Notes on the Composers and Their Works

Franz Schubert (1797-1828) often mentioned as the first lyric poet of music, was one of the great melodists of all time. Unequaled as a composer of songs, he left as well much superlative symphonic, chamber, and piano music. In addition to his sonatas, he excelled in creating new, smaller romantic forms such as the Impromptues, the Moments Musicaux. The outpouring of hundreds of lovely dance pieces from his pen: the Ländler, Waltzes, Ecossaises, etc. is nearly unparalleled. Of this rich heritage our foilio presents a fair sampling, negotiable even by players of modest technical means. Schubert did not furnish tempo marks for these dances or because the titles themselves gave clear indication of the desired tempo. The following brief survey will perhaps be helpful.

Minuet: graceful andantino.
Ländler: moderate, somewhat weighted tempo, with clear accents on downbeats.
German Dance: nearly identical with the Ländler.
Waltz, Walzer: somewhat lighter than the Ländler, having a more graceful lilt.
Ecossaise: French adaptation of a (supposedly Scottish) country dance in lively time.

A great deal of Schubert piano music, especially his dance have a melodic spontaneity, and almost improvisatory character, which should be reflected in performance. The enjoyment of this music, the savoring of every charming phrase, melodic turn, every harmonic surprise should be rendered with evident relish and idiomatic flair.

Robert Schumann (1810-1856) leading German composer of the Romantic era, one of the most original writers of piano music, acheived many stylistic innovations. He was also a critic of lasting integrity and lasting influence. His wife, Clara, one of the most prominent concert pianists of the nineteenth century, was his first important interpreter.

Schumann was the first of great masters who was inspired by the fantasy-world of children, their diversions and educational needs. He considered his "Scenes from the Chidren" as "reminiscences of an older person" and intended the titles of the individual pieces as "directions for the performances of the music." His later opus the "Album for the Young" he panned as a "Christmas Album" for his children, the composition of which gave him "indescribable joy."

Schumann's music for children, even the technically simplest ones, were always conceived and fashioned with masterful craftsmanship. These pieces often have a pronounced polyphonic texture, which is often overlooked and unrealized by young players, so that the carefully layered inner voices of the structure pass unnoticed. Examine, for instance the charming "First Loss," or especially the lovely "Reverie" which projects its simple, enchanting melody in a strict, four-part, sophisticated harmonic texture. Performers have to be keenly aware of this, so the interplay of voices will properly support and enhance that immortal strain.

Schumann notated his piano works with utmost care and in unfailing detail as to tempo, phrasing, dynamics, all of which should be carefully observed.

Felix Mendelssohn-Bartholdy (1809-1847) a leader and idol of musical Germany in mid-nineteenth century, famous not only as composer, pianist and organist, but also as the first star-conductor in the annals of music. His creative precocity was unparalleled. His "Overture" to "A Midsummer Night's Dream," a masterpiece by any standards, or age group was written when he was seventeen. He excelled in most other fields of music (except opera)–his symphonies oratorios, and chamber music are still staple concert items today.

The core of his keyboard output is represented by the 48 "Songs Without Words," which are the depository of a wealth of lyric invention and finely honed pianistic delights. Sensitive, well-articulated melody playing is the single, most important factor in the performance of Mendelssohn's piano music, which is almost entirely homophonic (melody with accompaniment). Its characteristic structure is a top-line melody, singly or in thirds, supported by chords or other subordinate parts. It is usually a three-tier texture: melody, bass, and inner voices. The player's task is to recognize and properly balance these three components according to the familiar hierarchy of sound: the melody line dominates, closely coordinated in volume with the bass part and both supported more discreetly by the inner voices and figurations. Remember: the most elementary aspect of romantic pianism, the production of fine, singing tone, involves the application of varying degrees of arm-weight.

Contents

Franz Schubert

Robert Schumann

Felix Mendelssohn-Bartholdy

Two Ecossaises

Franz Schubert

1.

2.

Three Ländler

Franz Schubert

1.

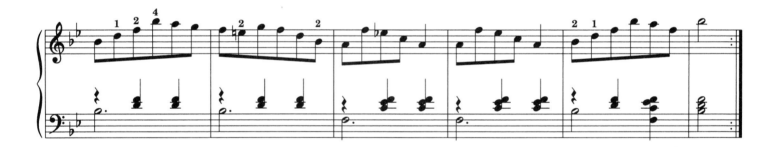

2.

Two Comic Ländler

Franz Schubert

1.

*repeated sections may be played an octave higher in both hands

2.

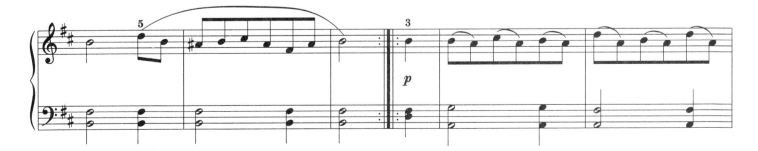

Walzer from Graz *

Franz Schubert

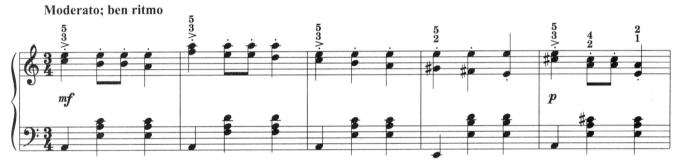

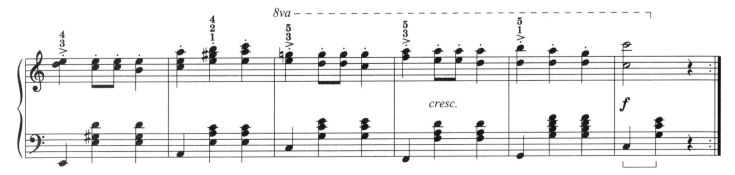

* *Graz is the second largest city in Austria*

Three German Dances

Franz Schubert

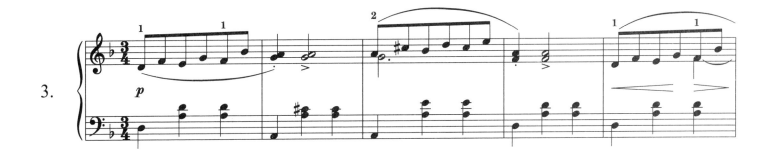

3.

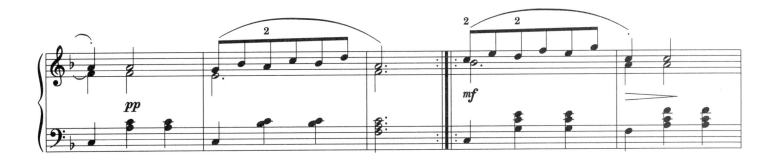

Menuett and Trio

Franz Schubert

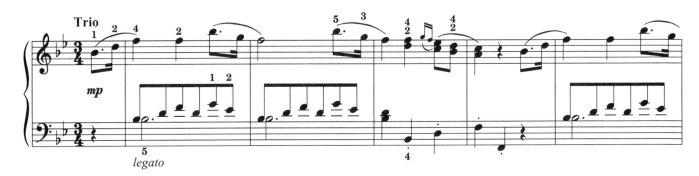

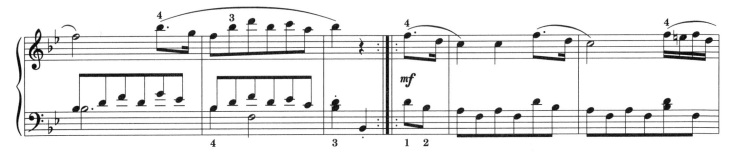

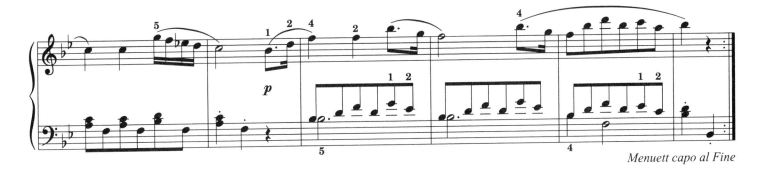

Menuett capo al Fine

Valse Sentimentale

Franz Schubert

Four Walzer

Franz Schubert

1.

2.

3.

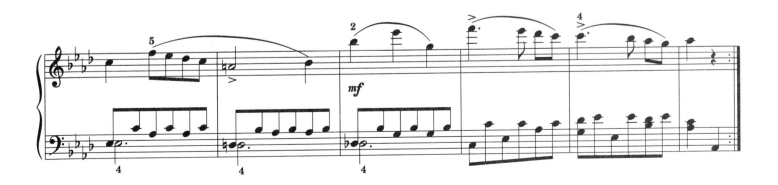

4.

Waltz

Franz Schubert

Scherzo
(Op. posth.)

Franz Schubert

Allegretto

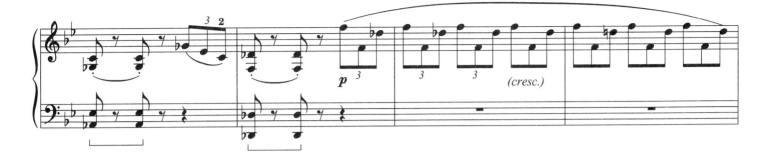

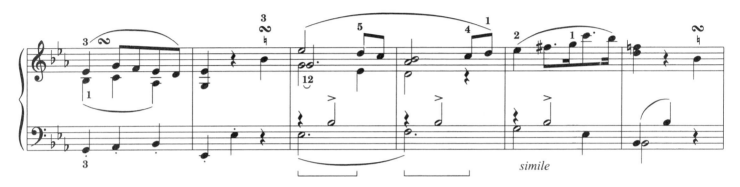

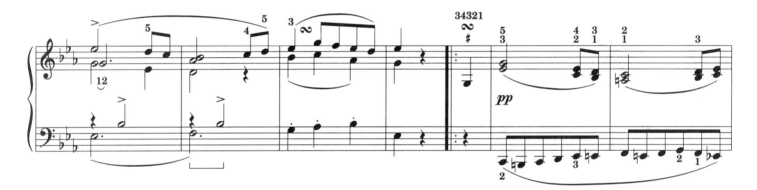

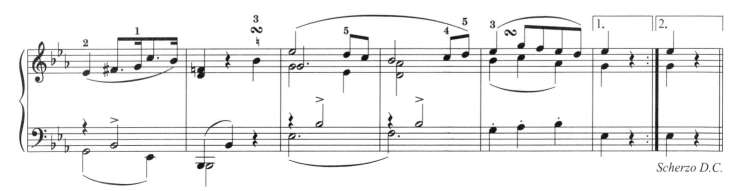

Scherzo D.C.

Moment Musical
Op. 94 No. 1

Franz Schubert

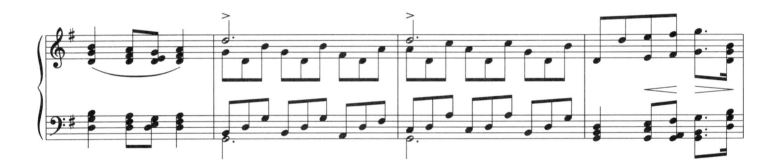

Moment Musical
Op. 94, No. 3

Franz Schubert

(staccato sempre)

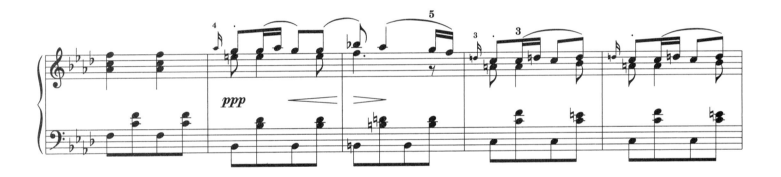

Moment Musical
Op. 94, No. 5

Franz Schubert

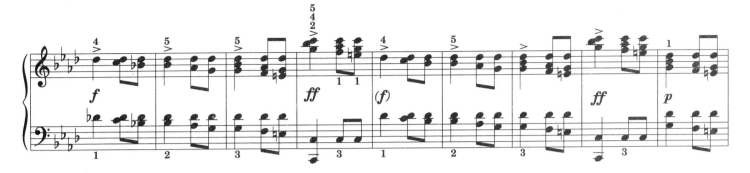

Impromptu
Op. 142, No. 2

Franz Schubert

Allegretto
sempre ligato

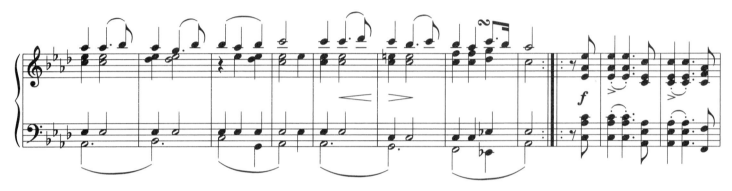

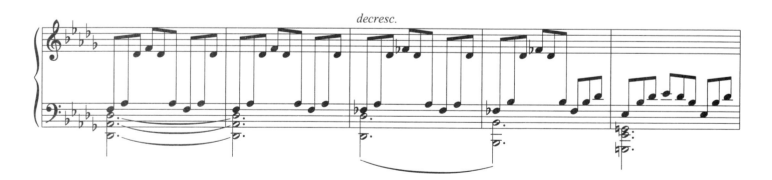

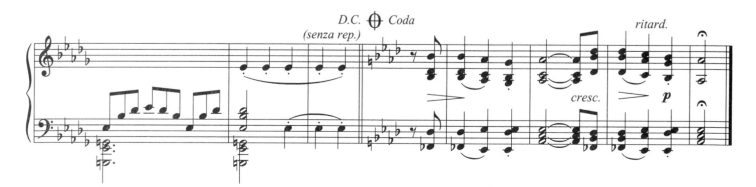

Bear Dance

from the sketch book for "Album for the Young," Op. 68

Robert Schumann

Little Piece
Op. 68, No. 5

Robert Schumann

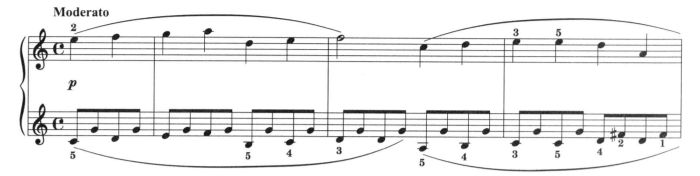

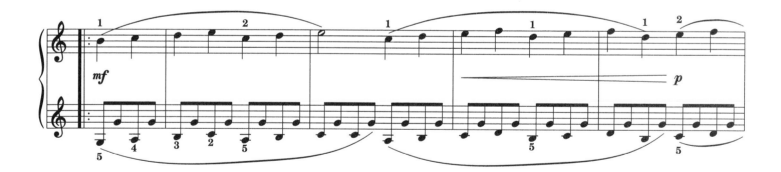

The Wild Horseman
Op. 68, No. 8

Robert Schumann

First Loss
Op. 68, No. 16

Robert Schumann

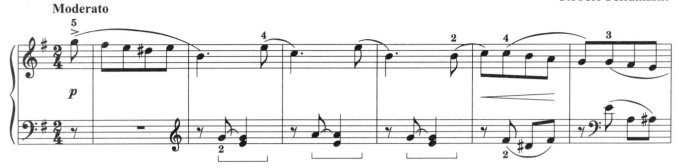

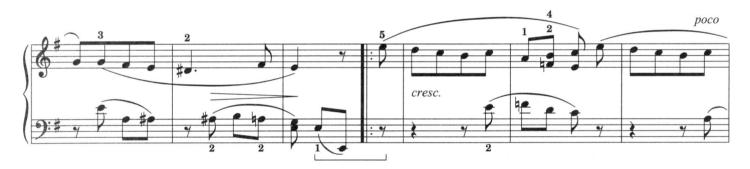

The Poor Orphan
Op. 68, No. 6

Robert Schumann

The Hiding Cuckoo

from the sketch book for "Album for the Young"

Robert Schumann

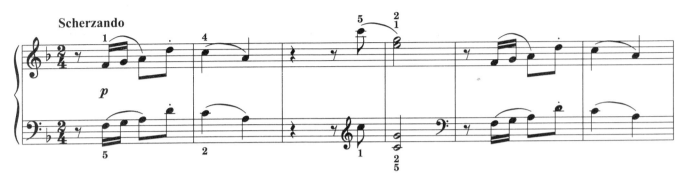

Merry Farmer Returning from Work

Op. 68, No. 10

Robert Schumann

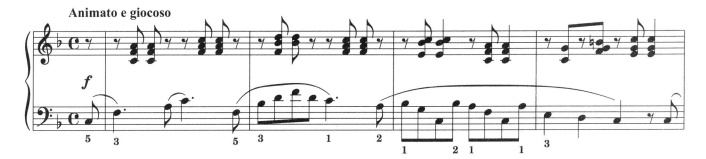

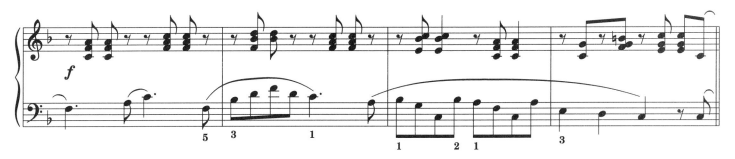

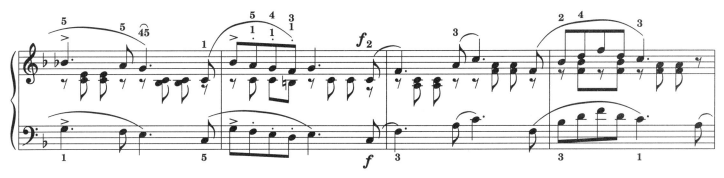

Blindman's Buff

from the sketch book for "Album for the Young"

Robert Schumann

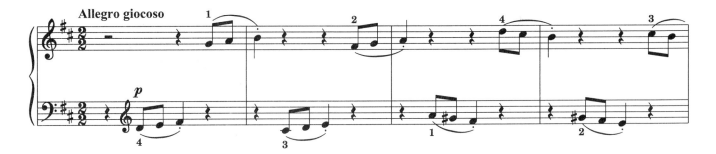

Album Leaf
from Op. 99, "Colored Leaves"

Robert Schumann

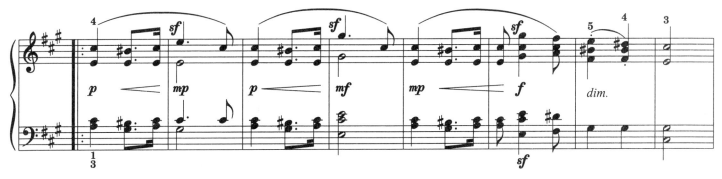

Cradle Song

Robert Schumann

Hunting Song

Op. 69, No. 7

Robert Schumann

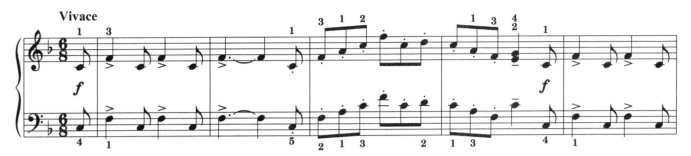

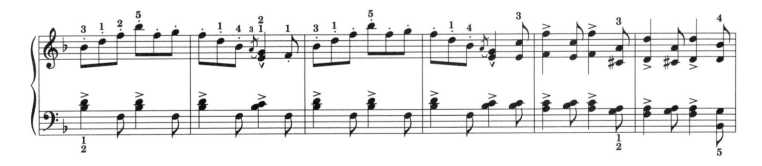

The Reapers' Song

Op. 68, No. 18

Robert Schumann

Allegretto

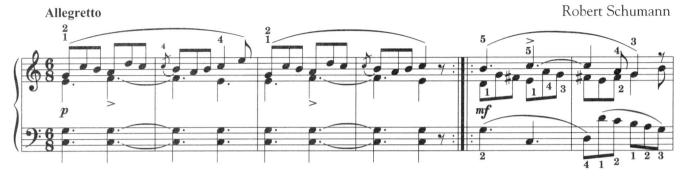

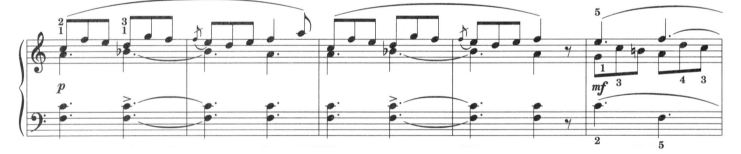

About Strange Lands and People

Op. 15, No. 1

Robert Schumann

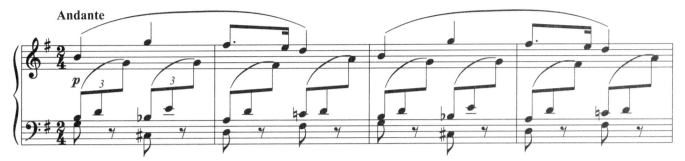

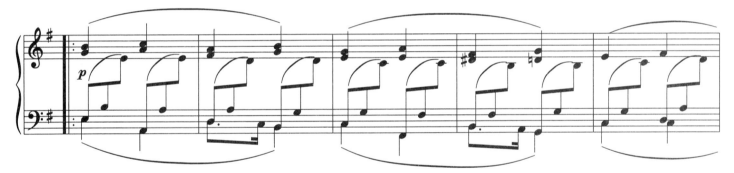

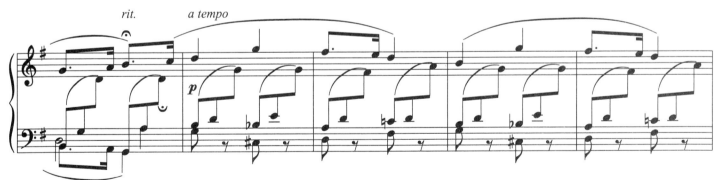

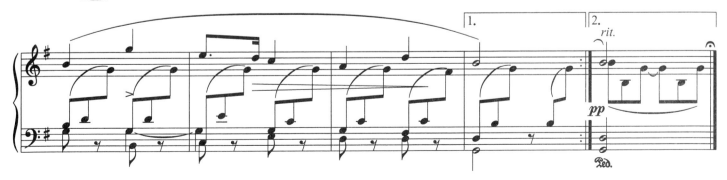

Norse Song
Greeting to G*
Op. 68, No. 41

Robert Schumann

In the style of a folk-song

* Niels W. Gade (Danish composer and friend of Schumann)

Harvest Song
Op. 68, No. 24

Robert Schumann

Lively
with cheerful expression

Theme with Variations

From Op. 118, "Sonatas for the Young"

Robert Schumann

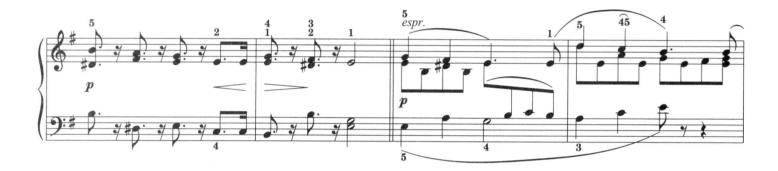

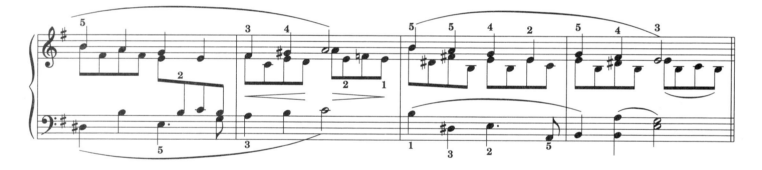

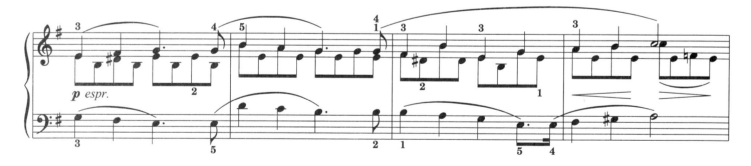

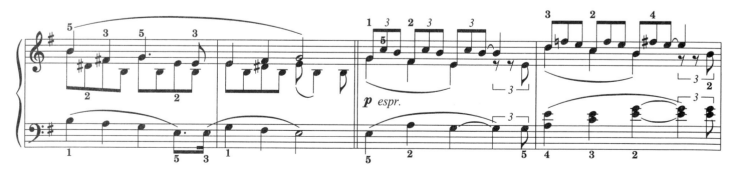

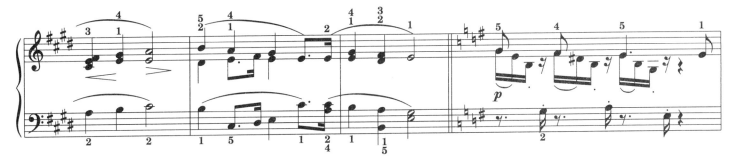

a tempo

A little slower

Sonata for Children

Op. 118, No. 1, First Movement

Robert Schumann

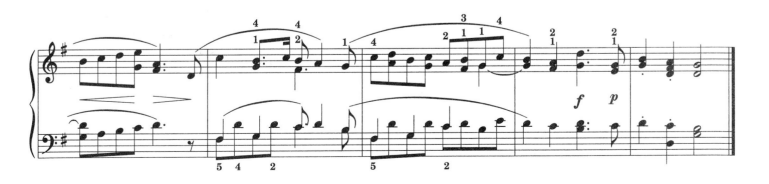

Italian Sailors' Song

Op. 68, No. 36

Robert Schumann

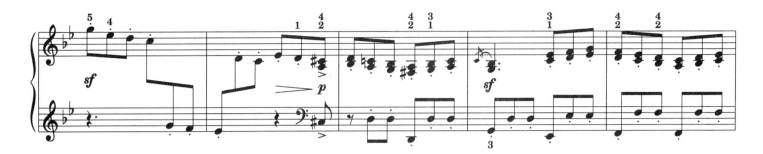

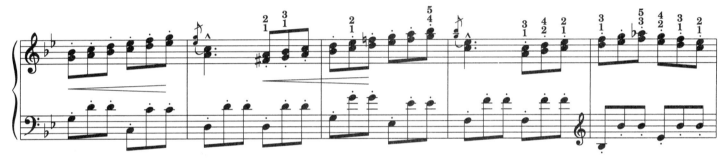

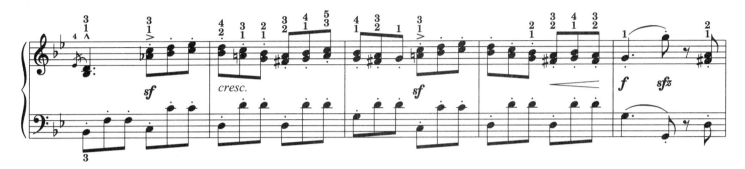

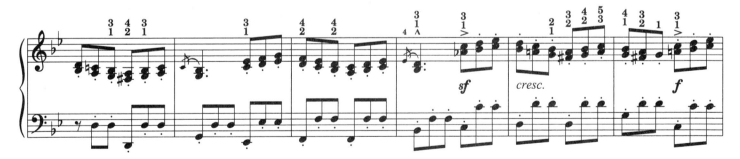

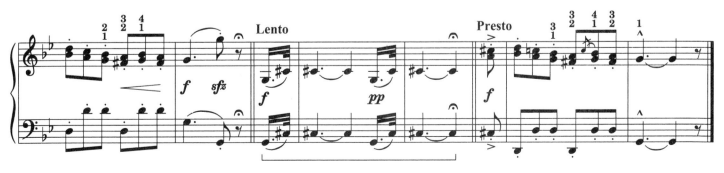

Child Falling Asleep

Op. 15, No. 12

Robert Schumann

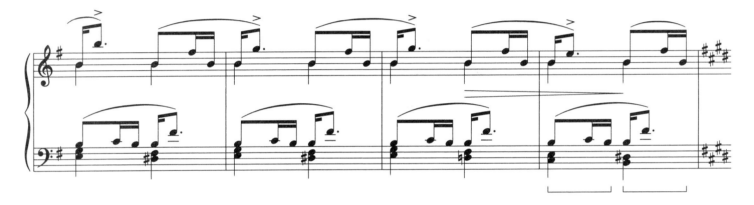

Reverie
Op. 15, No. 7

Robert Schumann

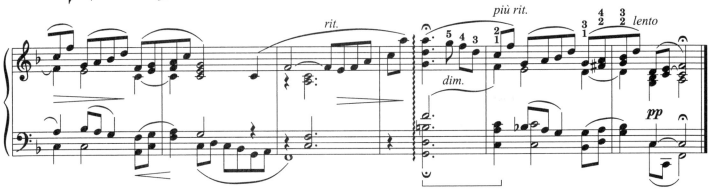

Folk Song

Op. 68, No. 9

Robert Schumann

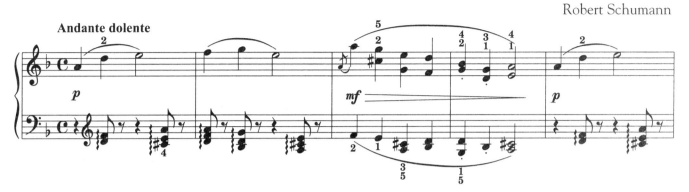

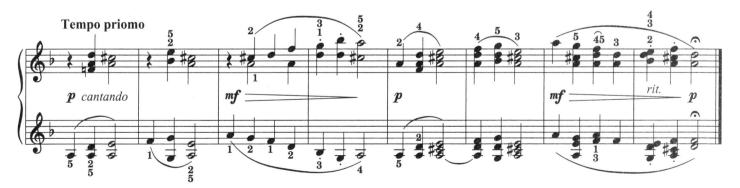

Friendly Landscape

from Forest Scenes, Op. 82, No. 5

Robert Schumann

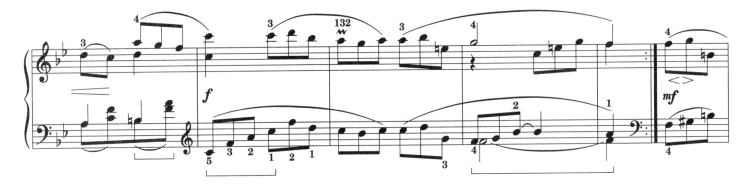

At the Fireside
Op. 15, No. 8

Robert Schumann

Allegretto grazioso

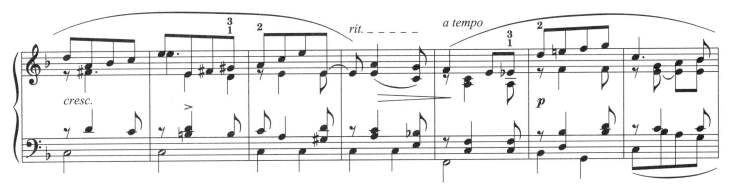

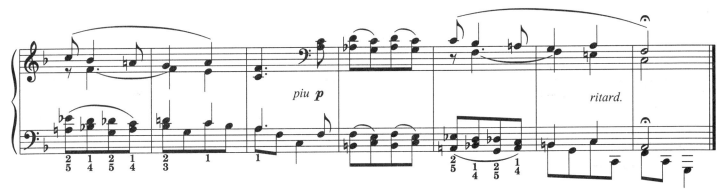

Romanze

Felix Mendelssohn-Bartholdy

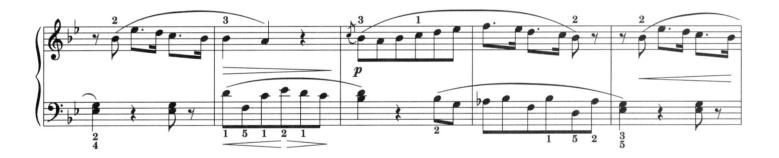

Peasant Song

Felix Mendelssohn-Bartholdy

Poco sostenuto

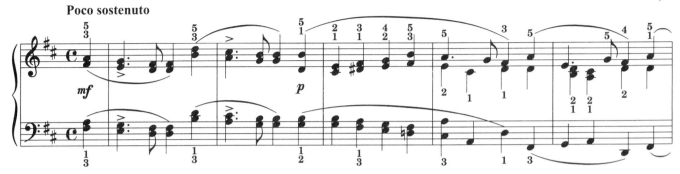

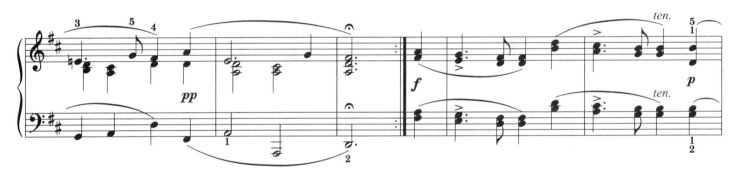

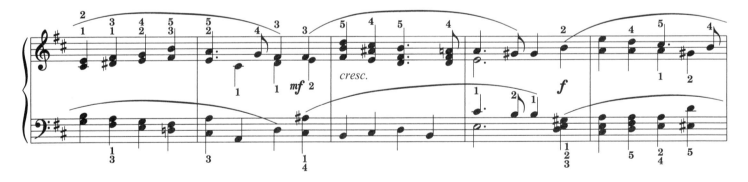

Song Without Words

Op. 30, No. 3

Felix Mendelssohn-Bartholdy

Adagio non troppo

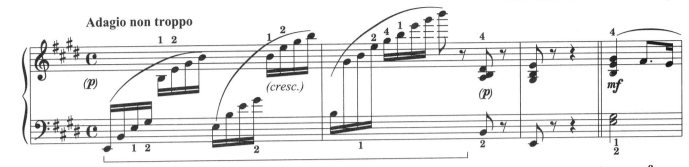

Song Without Words
Op. 19, No. 4

Felix Mendelssohn-Bartholdy

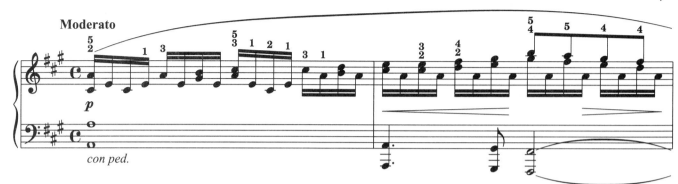

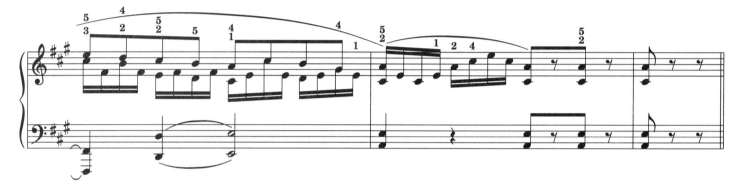

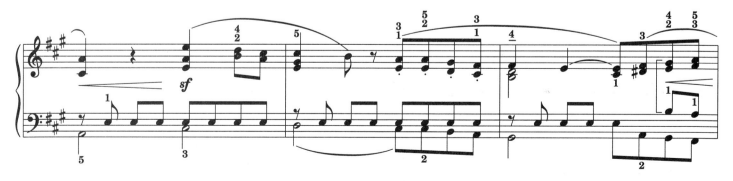

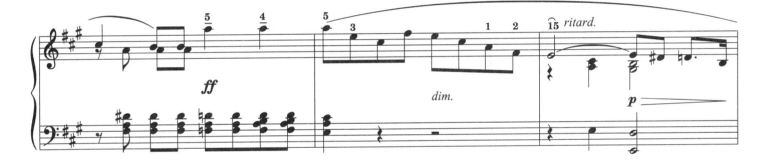

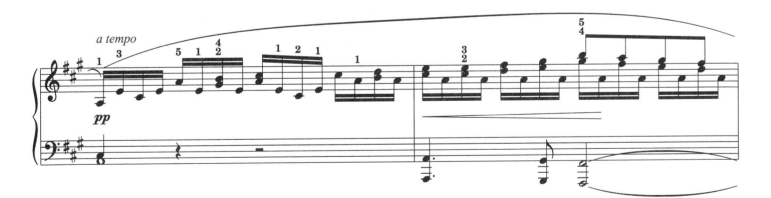

Venetian Boat Song

Op. 30, No. 6

Felix Mendelssohn-Bartholdy

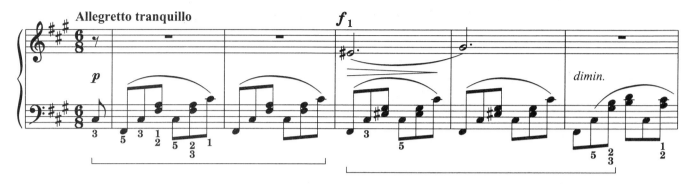

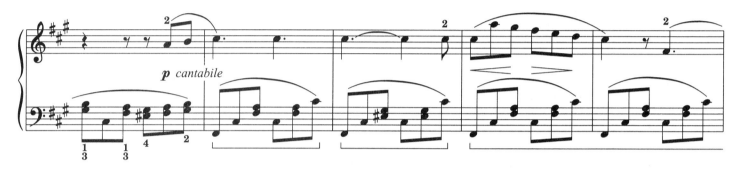

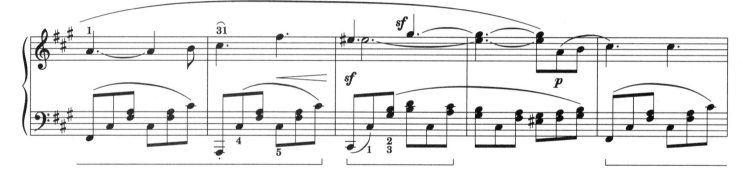

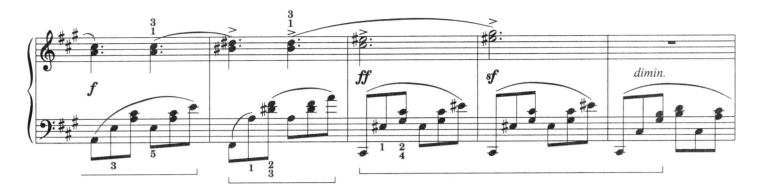

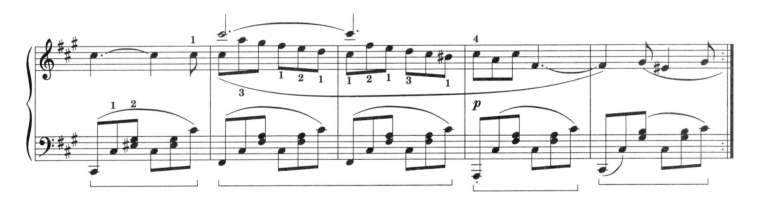

Funeral March

Op. 62, No. 3

Felix Mendelssohn-Bartholdy

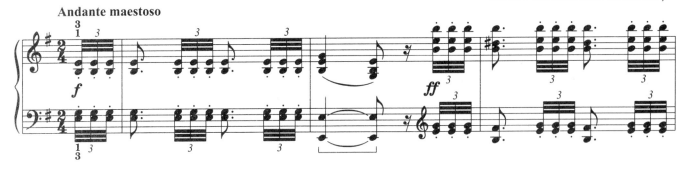

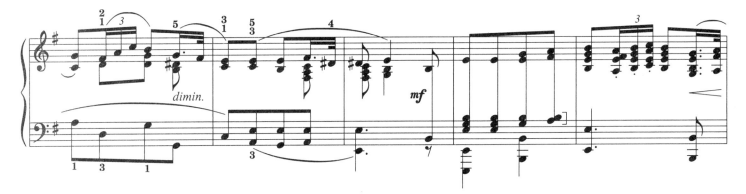

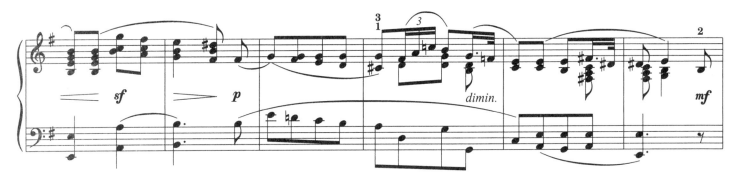

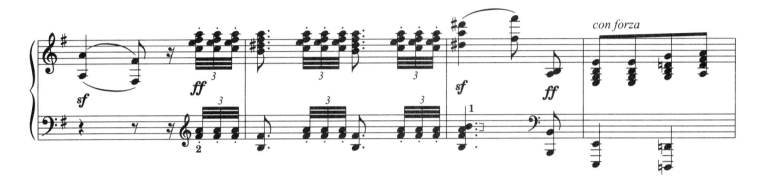

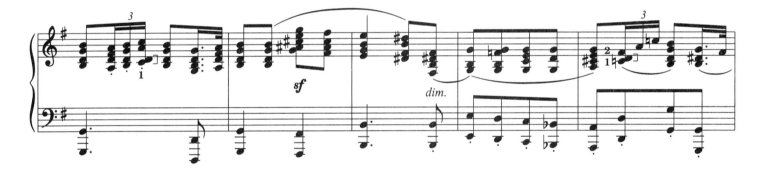

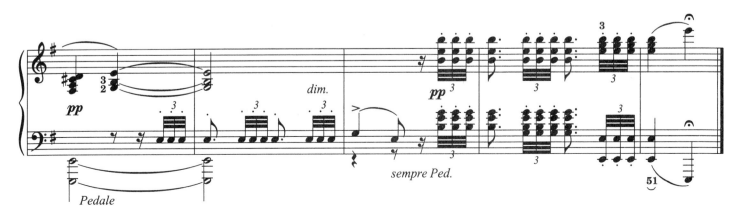

Boat Song

Felix Mendelssohn-Bartholdy

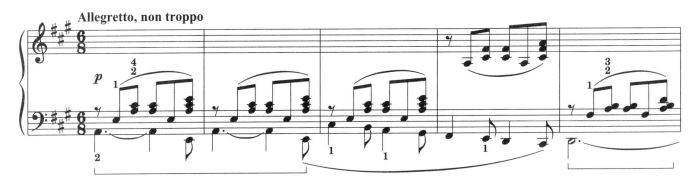

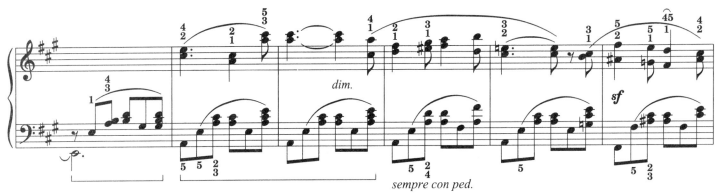

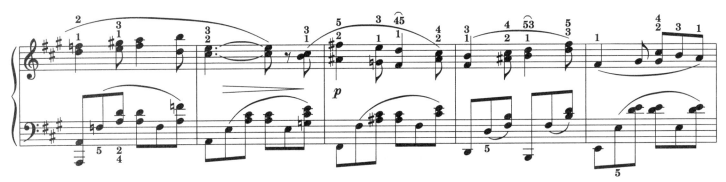

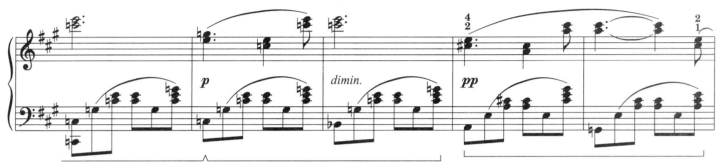

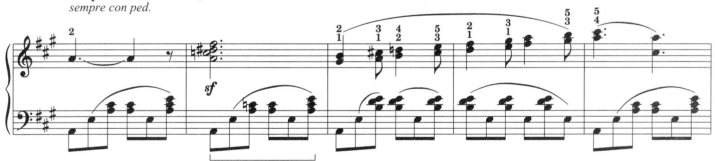

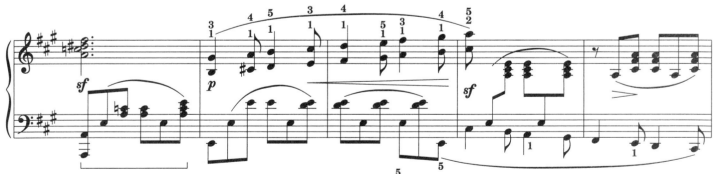

Children Piece

Op. 72, No. 2

Felix Mendelssohn-Bartholdy

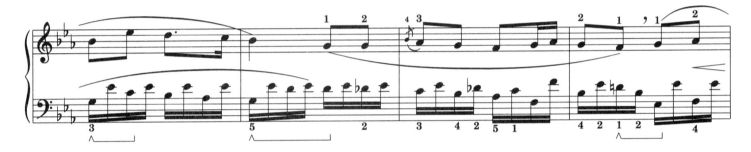

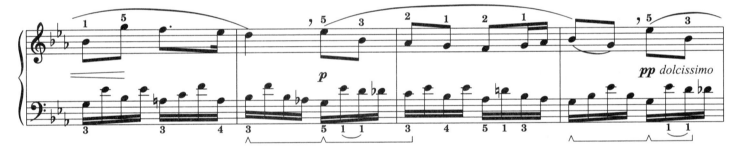

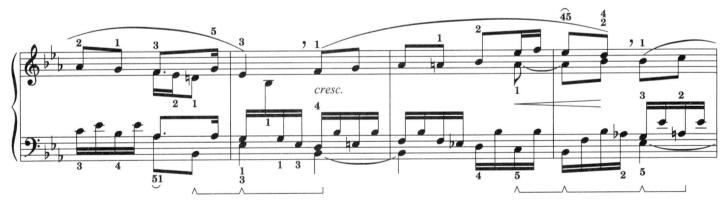

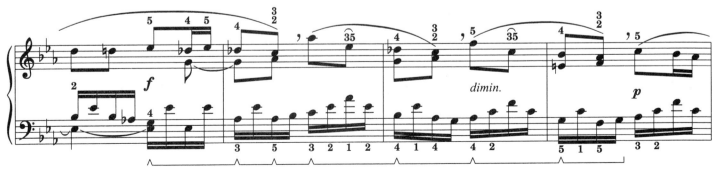

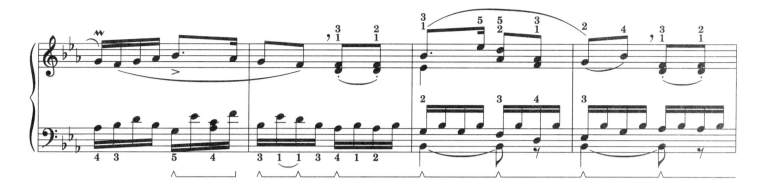

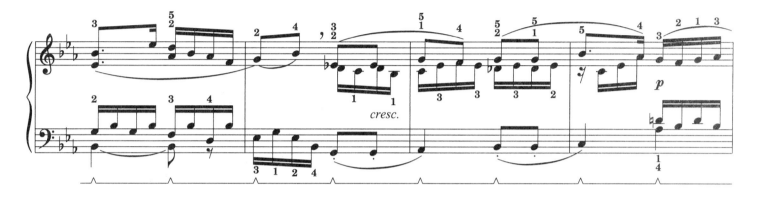

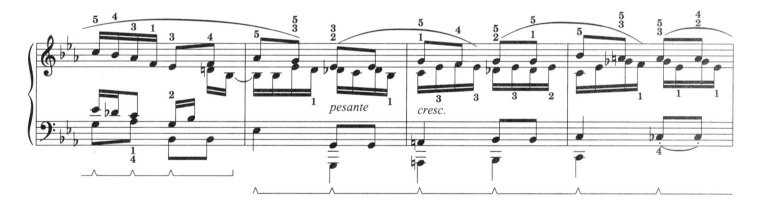

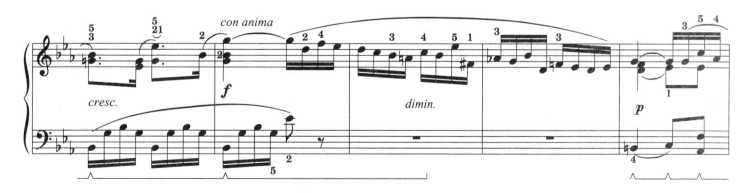

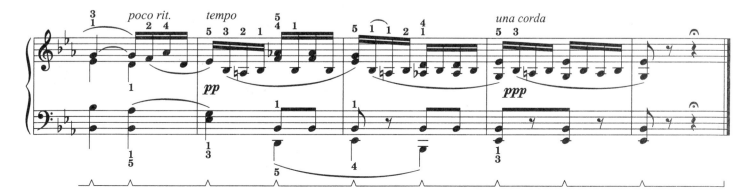

Character Piece
"Softly, with Feeling"
Op. 7, No. 1

Felix Mendelssohn-Bartholdy

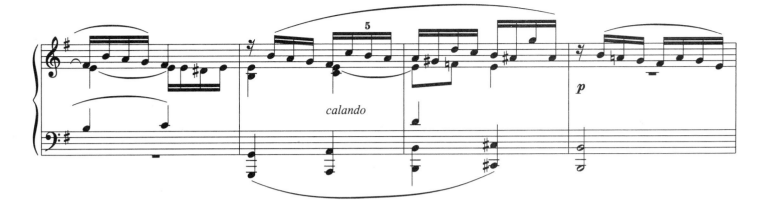

Children's Piece
Op. 72, No. 1

Felix Mendelssohn-Bartholdy

Allegro moderato

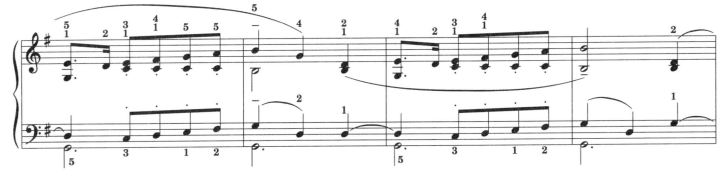

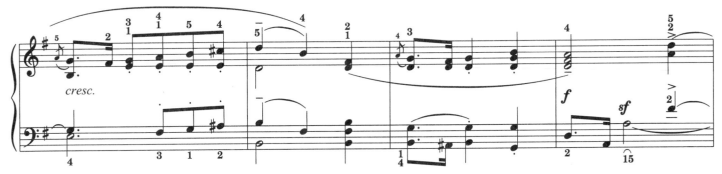

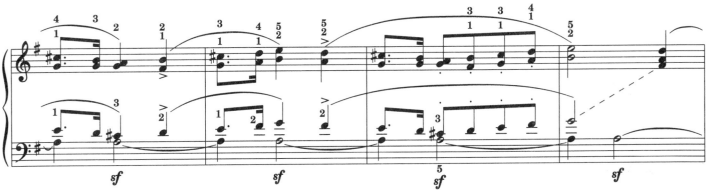

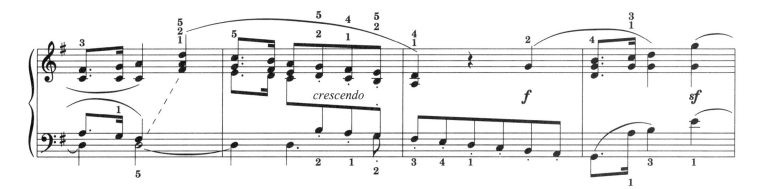

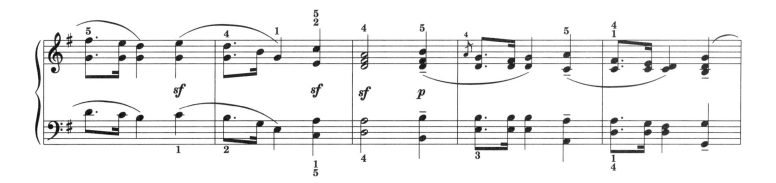

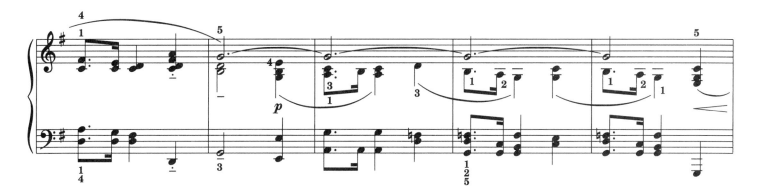

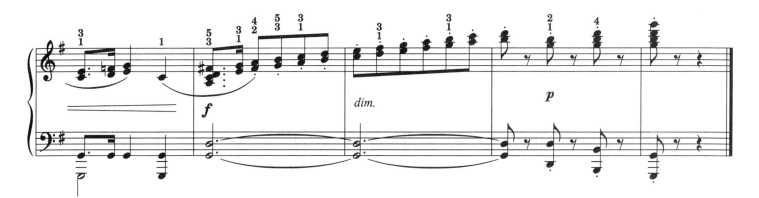

Song Without Words

Op. 102, No. 3

Felix Mendelssohn - Bartholdy

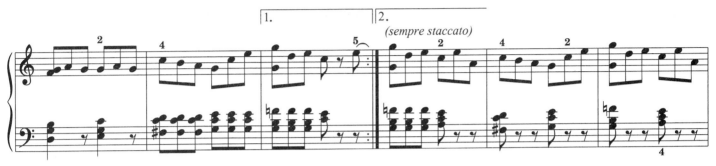

Song Without Words
Op. 19, No. 2

Felix Mendelssohn - Bartholdy

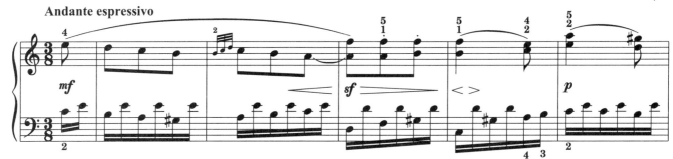

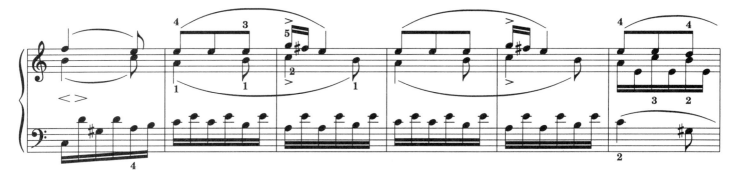

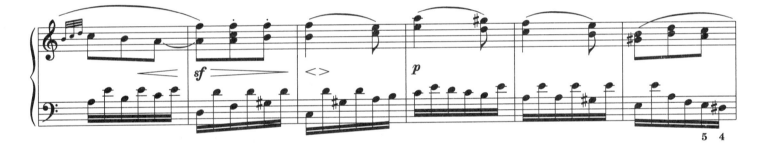

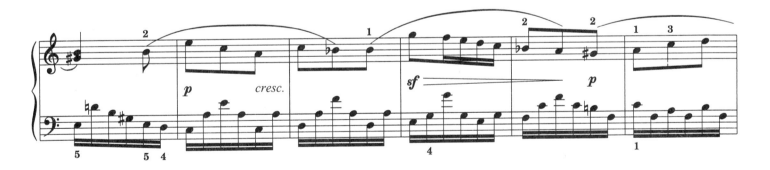

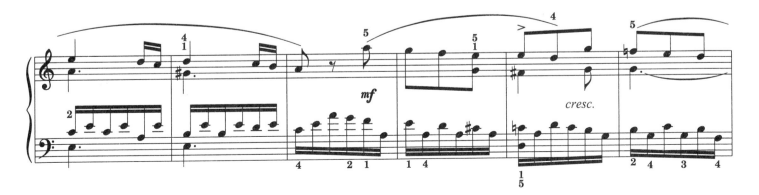

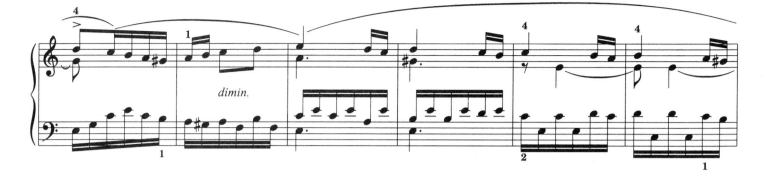

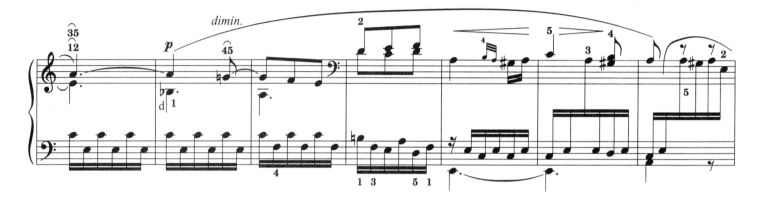

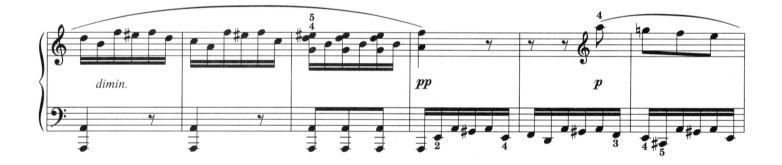

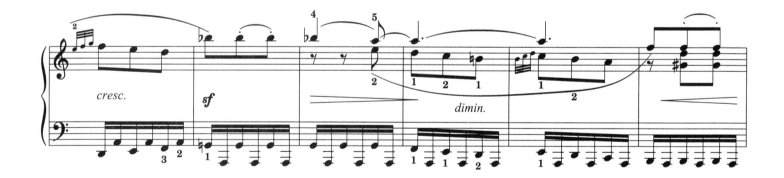

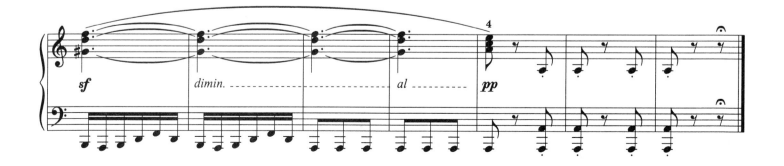